DEDICATED TO,

MY LOVING PARENTS,

        MANJUNATHA SWAMY

        VIJAYALAKSHMI

"My parents taught me how to face the world when failures occur and society taught me how failures were."

ABOUT HE BOOK AND AUTHOR,

The book deals with success behind every failure one goes through in life starting from the state of failing in exams to failing in series of circumstances in life. The book typically explains the grief of a person when hit by back to back failures and gives a road to hit back the act and confess, it is very important to have failures in life. The author is one among those authors who stated with failing in engineering and came with a book to tell the world how it feels like being a shadow of failure in life and to the society.

- BHUVAN

Author

Days of Results

Papers flying all over the room, fingers conquering the giant Google and the moment left undecided. From dusk to dawn all the chartings are molded with wild guesses "what would be his future?" The road is clear from a student to think what he has done and what he will be in his future. During this auspicious day of each student many try down the valley of faith which is not just a ray of hope but ray of eternal ability, which often the actual student gets lost. It will be never an easy going to handle the pressure which is never felt and this prepares us from the boom pressure mode which waits in the illusions of future. The basic starts from here when your parents offering ample amount of gifted teachings but the intensity varies depending on the grade one pursues. The idea of results is good enough and now the climax gets into the role "I FAILED, I FAILED", that moment is time of tears feels like everything in this world has ended. Faith that is the only tool that prevails still gets frozen and this time it will be on the time of peace. This crucial movement of each student gives rise to an extreme dramatic change under extreme conditions; back the well of disappointment, may be every student thinks he/she is the dumbest and weakest of all. It's never a time to argue or beat upon the bush when you are under pressure and all eyes are open on you. The only soul which is pure for true good fortune stays calm and thinks "BILL GATES is my god father" never less a piece of marks card could change his time and time could not touch him when he threw it in heaven. The worst performance calls you down when those eyes with expectations see the face as a convicted assault. Feeling this way was all over in life when Google brought me the page which I never wanted to see again, the roads of hopes flying all across the terrace of house trying to escape to space from the poor reality of life.

I was always taught "where there is a will there is a way". I raised myself in a critic where all see me as a criminal and I see them as cops surrounding me even though I didn't kill anyone but myself my inner will. Felt as if the sun too didn't want to see me anymore, he went down, it was evening now nothing could stop me from thinking those ways which were never my way travelling through the dark sided life as though I was possessed by evil of dead faith. It was a battle between for light in dark, safely I turned my face to light when I felt results are time changers not life changers. The clock turned at the night wearing a mask of 8, now had to be present for timely food which even had to be finished in deadly silence. Night was a sorrow of light even the stars failed to show them up, all round the night sleep was unfortunate every seconds feels like an hour, the feel of disappointment and helplessness was at its height. Started gazing the roads through a tiny window just beside the room, the great destiny nightmare turned out to be goose bumps and mental health was rotating up and down the clock that night, only a half day sleep was adjustable and proceeded.

Days of Plight

Mean while, it is sentencing the feeling of a student is like assuming fish out of water. The next day's coming up are days of rotating decisions, where the soundings "what were your grades?" "Which class?" "Which rank?" these words literally torture and beats the will power of an individual. All the days and nights feel baseless, why were they above all after even when I failed, this was the real marks feel it, it's the epic meaning even though I was failed, day and night never changed just because of a mark on the transcript, the nature backs you up with encouragement. Be patient the nature gives you break nevertheless you are a high graded, average graded or low graded all are same and equal before the nature.

Middle of the day everything seems alright after a 24 karat struggle to listen each and every words of the elders, eyes were raised above and playback starts those days when never knew the meaning of early morning, sun raised to woke up and songs woke up. In the mid day impulse to show appearances was difficult task, when all the further dreams were ruined up. Mind is blind and thinks of unnatural ways to be a super natural once again, grades were all removed, the mind filtering thoughts of grades and rank it dreams to be a vampire riding on society thoughts. Reminder every time accompanying those dreams vengeance to prove something that was resemblance of the future. The thoughts are so rouge that it brings the feeling of Hitler in mind. The one of the saddest is when your own parents feel my child is weak and their feelings for their children first and student next, those very troubling words "please study we got nothing than knowledge" in a student's point of view it feels so pity on those words from the bottom of their heart praying for the well being of there son/daughter to stand still in the society. There is a noticeable link between the parents and the society; it is so clear that parents officially live for the society and wish their children to acquire the best possible status in the un-transparent society. Of course parents in the typical Indian style always want their children to be doctors or engineers, yes that's definitely not bad, not at all as they wished you to be at the top most position no one in this apparent world cannot rule out these words and feelings.

Clouds move in the directions as they wish, when non-living phenomena is so powerful in moving towards its needs, a universal super power human Cant.? As simple as that when you like your profession and desire to work, that moves things and when you get what you desire its much known truth i.e. miracles does happen, many of them posses an idea of choosing what they didn't know and even go on to the judgments of the public. A clever clear cut selection of what one has to be is indication of his/her heart and soul in individual's progress. Bachelor of Medicine is no longer great when it comes to geography or history of the earth and Bachelor's of Arts is no longer great when it comes to neutrality of the human body, every field has its own identity and vetches which can't be measured by photogenic individuals. Finally a failure of what you could not will be blamed on what they gave you.

"AN INTELLIGENT MAN MAKES HIS OWN DECISION, AN IGNORSNT MAN TAKES THE PUBLIC OPINION" – Chinese Proverb

A further explanation of these great words would be a game of foolishness.

Isolation Point

"They come, they go, they bring, and they take". The strongest wave of relatives lays the human identification, when marks cards wearing thick black dresses they bring back those which they told they always had. When failure gets charmed, it is the success waiting on the back for chance to show up so failure is not down, its success up. Fearing the old custom to worry for those who questioned you about your career will be hit straight by words "Watch me" they take back your name for publishing but this is not for official.

Hiding somewhere when relatives, friends come searching like a warranted criminal to know the truth of marks did panic, running for athletics will be all the way of a good failure, because that is the condition where one is masked to be prey for others. The era changes guts roaring around, standing still like an attentive soldier, heads high "I failed" believe you are no less than a soldier fighting at the border, he's fighting for the country and you are fighting for yourself. The electromagnetic induced energy keeps spinning with confidence, speak this: You're not less than any success I will chase it down. Staying out of focused for time of isolation breaks the will and ideal mind gives ways to untreated possessiveness.

Home that never leaves the mind to travel out of it in consciousness of the society provoking sentences causing rich depression. Many a times home becomes the point of isolation where failure takes the rest, following the worries of the outside world. Staying back at home considering him/her self to be the sin nest person alive takes away all the words of pain in mind and scientifically a rich source gives the answer taking a risk at mind losses memory pack cells and for real the person gets to be the worst than ever. After the entire person admires the people around him/her to be friendly and group him among the normal individuals for not considering him to be having done any sin.

The fatal arrangement around crushing the will power of a failure brand is nothing more than bubble on water. Those heart breaking questions "Why are you back home? "Why are you not going to school or college?" of course questioning is always right and no one can call it a wrong step but it is very much wrong when he/she knows why that person was staying back at home for a long time, may these known set up kind enquiry gives them joy of questioning and taunting literally but the person who goes on listening to those will no longer be human to answer them all. The human psychic point is very low compared to the other living organisms, when one leaves out of control to his feelings it is much difficult than performing a exorcism. The failure charmer is always a fortunate child may be others don't see that as, but believe the five fingered destiny creator in you, it does give many chances for those it feels good and favorite. Being home sick is often discouraged and sitting back in a room convincing you to be the end of all that happened is very much wrong "AN EMPTY MIND IS A DEVIL'S WORK SHOP".

There is nothing wrong in being home sick but staying alone in a filmy style of set repenting for what you have done goes to be very disastrous, mean while be a sufficient learner, pull out all the feelings of a winner bring back the energy, drive crazy and associate yourself to be the happiest. Every winner (Failure) is not the reason for what he/she is suffering from failures, the term failure is comparatively very less in life if it is taken in case of failing in exams, the much better failures are bouncing around the walls of life which are giants for exam failures, there you are not a given a year time to come back prepared. It is do or die.

Critical Crises

Making a choice in life is very important as air for lungs, often there is a mentality among the youth of India that the stream source opted by many has a good future and very successful, and the rest streams are cheap and done by some burden youths. There is a sad demise of these feelings inside a youths mind, very much sad to be informed that an individual selects his/her future based on the family status and pride accordingly a high paid streams of education is considered to be a matter of prestige and standard of life. If that was a case **DR. B.R AMBEDKAR** would have not been among the drafter of our country and DR. **APJ ABDUL KALAM** would have not been the greatest scientists India had ever seen. May be sometimes or often parents have a important role in shaping the future of their children, in a hurry burry life they wish ,it would be better and good if everyone is settled fast but during this process of settlement the important pre-vital option is deciding what he/she wants to be in his/her own future. The future an individual chooses is their whole responsibility and that doesn't mean parents don't have any right in questioning them, this is what we call it as misunderstanding the concept of liberty, freedom and self decision. When you are sure about the future which he/she has decided to live in, it does not bare any justice until and unless they truly convince themselves all alone, for this you can't take your parents, friends and relatives because it's you, you alone in your future. When this stage of convincing yourself is a success it's like the automated teller machine   everything   everyone surrounding you is convinced. The informal format of choosing the source stream based on the public demand and advice is condemned for a **_FUTURIST_** when you know who you are and what are your elements, be a doctor. Think, does any disease worry you when you yourself a doctor of the well known disease, when you are sure of things going to happen with you in future no power can stop the will power of horse. For winner no course, no source, no opinion is found essential, no date, no power, no time is ahead when your capabilities are all known by yourself what else these elements do of ? When you know what you are, your capabilities, what your future is. The phenomena is as simple as your work, you do and there is an intensity of pressure and related since it is your own dream not others. All the happiness and pain are related only to you but these decisions are rarely observed in families but if that is the case, then never for sure don't watch it again just go on never turn back. This realistic idea is having a clouded approval for advantages in life, when you decide it's your whole heart and soul into that and you grow even better in dependent nature, face the world, face the pain, know the struggle. Being a decisive minded individual and looking alike the horse view which is a narrow site that never sees what's going on around, it is safer until you have no goals and aims being a **FUTURIST.** Being a free minded individual it is always acceptable. Individual tries his new stuffs, new ideas, being practical, realistic. Struggling is the only path which is determined for any group may be toppers or weaker all though struggle is well known for toppers and it is also a word never known before for the so called failures until date, being a struggler in his/her own way of source is path towards enlightment not only towards marks.

It would be not wrong to confess that if you go in the path you always wished to, the journey will be never a burden and never will it be a silent one beating the silence of death. The more the journey comprise of, it gives the faith in one's own work and caliber which he/she never knew about, taking this challenge is not always as the easiest ever imagined since it is mentioned about the difficulties to overcome, but once it is done life is all yours may you be thrown with a payment of heavy perk. But remember you will be no longer living the life your parents had always wished to, to be a father's son or daughter attending college dusk to dawn, having a heavy pay back achieving those dreams which your dad dreamt of, but caution this situation can be surplus among the artistic minded individuals.

TIME-DESTINY IS YOU..?

"Life never turns around when you try"

"Life never turns around when you die"

"Life ever turned when all the turns turned"

"Give the moment when all the turns leading hurricane, broke them with turns of paint"

"Manifestation of thoughts bring lights when dark side row was among the nearest ones"

"Be a person of vengeance when it comes to will, when it comes to dreams, when it comes to teachings"

"Right is all yours when all the things of your dreams are others"

"Give a smile when I was dark, when I was tidy and when it was that pendulum with sounds gave slaps on"

"Although we are Homo sapiens, we killed each other, each wish; it was dawn which we all cried"

"Make that pendulum around those five fingered almighty and say destiny I am your creator".

There is a typical term for Indians are concerned when a son/daughter opts his career in creative field, the usual style of father opinion is "what would you do after that? "Would you get a government job for that? And many often decide themselves confessing it's not a bachelor's at all, this can be explained by a simple reason i.e. un-updated source of mind. We weaving in the 21st century and today no creative innovators ears no less than any government official and so called backbone professional of the country. For a very simple example would be defining, A person choosing animation as his career and it would be described as a non degree stream which does not hand over the degree certificate at the end of course. Think does it make sense naming it as Bachelor of Science in Animation and possessing no bachelorette, would there be an institution named ICAT being top most in Indian standards offering it with an intake of only 20 students per year and placing its students in the top companies. It would be amazing to know that a famous character named Chota Bhem has a turnover of 40cr. This would be sufficient to confess anyone you are wrong.

Does it make sense to address everyone to be an IAS or IPS officer and dreaming everyone to have government jobs? Every individual has a noticeable different interest and caliber, everyone don't dream to be a civil servant or doctor there are lot more people living, if that was a case India would not have thinkers, philosophers and artist who raised up Indian flag above all telling the world ask us what we don't have.

Of course in India a person who opts for a career other than professional stream are treated no less than terrorist. Straight goal straight vision and straight choice emerges to be skills in each individual, bring it when it is told no more it can be kept.

Cloning Negativity

When everything goes wrong the human mind is engineered in such a way to think never about everlasting freedom. Brimming with joy when everything was right and deep condolence when everything was wrong, many often testimony their wishes when failures turn out to be boom. Cloning negativity inside one's mind is rapid when the burden of pressure builds on an ever calm mind, trying to convey those hard feelings of pressure one does choose relaxing themselves in ultra negative processed thoughts. As mentioned failures in exams are much not considered important in life since marks are not life, it's just a part of life. A proverb timed when all the doors are closed not less than a window is open to see the world from that point. The common time when doors are closed is one goes himself pledging to the addictions which is imprinted, where not only failures destroy; the addiction destroys their own kind. Passionately claiming for suffering caused in life and curing it means of most usual strain: Smoking, Boozing starts when one feels I should be relaxed for moment and goes on for a time with one. As the used to it kind attitude sets up the functioning and number of intakes increases but rather self pressure does not in any penny. Mentioning the words cigarette, cigar could be encouraging the statement so as a form of concern it will be described as "IT". It takes on the charge of body like a major appointed, when the consumption of daily artificial regulated air starts, he feels he is relaxed but neither knows he is slow poisoned by the air with which he decided to live on. Some even though doing the injustice to self possessed try with boozing, pacifying the drink, all these mentioned crises to human nature are disastrous. Let us get confirmed sapiens of this universe; no one is born rich or poor, weak or strong, intelligent or dumb. Everything holds you and your will, let pressure ever last it is also a source of entire combustion to theories of life. When there is an opposition force resisting you, it would be fun holding it back and moving on. Remember one track of line "You may live without opponents but you cannot win without opponents". Racing ahead of these there are negligible group which defines the end of this world just because of their failure, if that was a case would this country needed Jan Lokpal Bill? If those had repented for their mistakes. The group of individuals can be inspired by biological terminology 'Suicide Bags', as the name suggest the work of this biological enzyme is when it lacks food it destroys its own kind, not too much differences can be found in humans too when wish never goes on the virtually be their own 'Suicide Bags'. Being suicide bags does it mean to a question to be raised, does it bother when others do that in front of you. Yes it does worry when your friend or relative suffers that, when their conditions persist keep the bet you would write a book on that. It is mu much difficult to know what the personality of yours decides to, but nothing is impossible to bring under your own custody. The world is large enough and sufficient for everyone's needs, sounds philosophical but true, a mind of soft nature turns out to be a suicide bag usually. In detail to be explained there exist two types of individuals namely soft minded and modest. The modest minded is easy going and easy explainable since you are reading the confession of the author since he is one among those, the soft's are individuals who exist in large number around the world. The capacity of tolerance to pain and gain is much less, a simple word that strings them can be found deep inside their heart. The worry is not modest as they posses care free nature and perturbed about things on going and smart enough not to take up any responsibility for anything that has happened which is very much appreciated in certain circumstances and fine handed. The soft's are as mentioned undergo all the criteria which does happen in large scale for them by them.

Being to doctor is a standardized comment but for sure one can make it good going by making them feel they are special and nothing is lost. Friends can make this very much success than parents; bring them to atmosphere where minded brains roam around which is more acceptable than prescription. Based on the lively observation and experience looking around there are certain Doing's and Don'ts when cloning negativity is at its peak:-

- ➢ Bring down the hobbies of firing talents within.
- ➢ Ring drums and songs only of joy.
- ➢ Keep up with all the electronic devices.
- ➢ Write a book like what the author did.

Don'ts:-

- Never look at this book.
- Never put your ear to pathos's.
- Never look at dark sided walls of life.

Be sure **"You are special and you are unique when it comes to face of life, you live like lion and not zebra."**

Failure Is Not a Sin

"Sin" the only word popping out a dozen times in all the religious texts present around the world. Sin- The unforgivable mistake committed by a human and mercy is condemned and the human shall be addressed to hell.

The perfect meaning and circumstances of sin can be explained by religious texts written centuries ago.

- ➢ One does not commit sin when he/she does know what the result of act performed is.
- ➢ One commits sin when he/she gets problems to others.
- ➢ One does commit sin when unmerciful acts are privileged.

Accordingly to certain scripts but basic idea of sin remains unaddressed into the scenario of life and failure.

When does a human perform a so called sin? Is it done when everything is alright? Exactly wrong, one does so called sin except the third notified law when one shall face the wrath of helplessness and bound by all the walls of dark entity of life. The fine theory here goes explaining the features of modern sin, when one does feel the power of being manipulated and pupated. Doing things which are unfamiliar and never thought of, when these credentials included in the phenomena of what else can a prophecy not tell, an all bound astrologer can predict the future then. When one does not know where he/she is travelling in a path of life with thrones and flowers, the question need an answer why does one lead to a path where it's   full of snakes? Of course no one dares to do that at present, everyone needs their life to be safe and preserved. Example is clean where does the question of knowing the future come around chipping here, when one individual is blindfolded and sent into a road of thorns, will it serve the purpose? The agenda remains never clarified, why fate chooses to manipulate such in-human psychology on humans. When one does not know what's happening, the first rule stating one does sin when he/she does know what the results were due to their act performed, it is unleashed here stating one cup of tea is necessary but " One drop of poison is Efficient " , no more caliber and pride needs and there comes to the un-leashment of the first promising Law , when the readers themselves don't know where they are and where they are peddling towards, no one possess the guilty of sin here then after. Soon after the first goes, there appears the apparent second: - One gets sin when he/she gets burdened problems to others. This basically strikes the mind; the right channel is here, the one who is pulled up with problems, will he himself tries to claim the ladder to find his own end?

When all the things around the apparent world is folded into a piece of mud and smoked into eyes, what else a person be told to do wonders, stabilizing the alternative a position around resisting itself the time from manufacture to death. Easily claimable to confess one who never knows what he/she is going through, how can they harm others? it would be seamless and funny that all the talks consists marks raising questions but unusually expecting the readers to answer those whether I was right or wrong. Successfully all the second law is cease fired believably. One and the least but never counting not the last of its kind, as it has its gigantic rule in all the medieval religious scripts as far as the topic is concerned.

 One gets send when the individual commits an un-merciful Act which is unforgiveable and repeatable, of – course the need the course of this theory is upholder by all the creations of the almighty. But the law is pretty summoned when almighty knows the walls of forgivable valency, why an individual does is performed to accept the fate. Fastest the train of life, no bridges and clamps, humans expect the cinematographic Spiderman to protect them. When success that keeps everyone happy and blooms roses can't possess the small life to the minute creature on earth, then how it's the smell of failures all around those red faces and start to leap the Poseidon. The ample amount of justification for life can be done here "When winner all yours, when failure you are none", that simple statement means a lot. When all the elements of life protecting yourself from all the neutrality would not be a sin but a failure is sin, you live all along the blood of humanity claiming to be the super power and failure is the only sin, you are recorded with all the criminal labeling and only failure is a sin. This kind of society that never witness any future out of a failure and one fine auspicious day it would be dooms day and they would say "Hey he was my neighbor, he failed but wow now he is something very Big" .

By the game of unfortunate fate and abuse by the fate one does not be labeled sin, and how it wasn't a crime act: You dint kill anyone or torture them, it is all you, yourself being killed. A successful note that brings by-pass of current is failure. Failure is absorbed by those who shape their own future. When one fails in life, he/she gets what was up there and will be successful in shaping own future standing tall. This situation is not possible when one goes on ride on horse of success which is blind and landing into a future of others, coming from zero to hundred in Nobel and starting from Hundred says the difference isn't it ?

A failure in life is as necessary as water to fish to shape a person made to live the life live and if that is a sin, then should be having sins, but only faith that matters.

THE EXPLAINABLE SIN

"It is, it is none other than those worried words"

"It is, the one with places all around one worries"

"It is, the only letter that blossoms those of the anciency"

"Keeping the time, guidance never revealed"

"Minimum of the most taken the greed of Human"

"Nevertheless the mind game and poisoned and fate "

"Three sins, three tones but where until the peace blows down"

"Mercy when taken, that given, brings even"

"Later   pendulum   running   time reeling"

"Game of Life turn his round and chase his wide till those all the hell break down "

"Sins done, sins underwent and rays timid "

"Sin grieve, sin touch lead led path of sun"

"Raining, althou raining when human in humanity down "

Intelligence of Wisdom Who Am I?

The same line as a typical politician dialogues "It is the face of two coins", one can never claim I have wisdom but no intelligence. This can't be the answer. Being scientifically updated one can define Intelligence as the sharpness of the human brain to perform series of acts and usually a genius is through potential to gain. Whereas wisdom is an in-built feature gifted to humans as for as the modern meaning is concerned, every single human being is born with wisdom.

Being practical the intelligence of a human is calculated by His/her marks in the recent past and IQ Level tests are no longer far today, when one is mounted with so much of intelligence and lacks to know what he/she has been for the recent past, would be a unlimited waste according to me. Every single child born on this earth would be presented with an enormous light called 'Wisdom'. **"Wisdom"**– An ancient script in the Latin addressing the knowledge of heaven. Being a part of modern world we don't address the same, but we call it as something which is preloaded necessarily to the human brains. Being brought-up to all the discussions one shall be with the question in mind, which has its first arrival to the human's wisdom or intelligence? The simple answer one can be given is wisdom and the proof shall be given is the discovery of fire and no preloaded intelligence ever humans had at that medieval past and a much better civilization existed. A quantity of intelligence related to the IQ Level is much amazing, that's often, felt by more people, than what they hear about wisdom, higher the IQ, Higher the Intelligence nearer to Albert Einstein and attempting to be compared among the nobles and to wear mask of others and so on. But one shall shoot a gazing star when whispered about the wisdom which has been never heard off.

"Ruler never loses his highness, but surely loses his kingdom"

A man born with an acquired caliber called intelligence can be lost but not the green wisdom.

It must be said the upper house of wisdom is intelligence and that's where intelligence hails from, a large scale invincible wisdom gives rise to mega term intelligence. One with wisdom shall conquer intelligence at his/her own potential when it's advanced and hard work combines giving out the term which is praised all over the world, an intelligence does not differ much than mathematics sincere too applies the law of "Practice makes man perfect" .

Wisdom is the mother of intelligence and all other knowledge, when one knows how to identify himself that can bring changes always revolved calling itself the revolution, one without wisdom is one without intelligence.

Often arguing about the generation of hyper tension conditioning the term ' They are no less brainless with the help of technology' , well it would be the nothing cooked out of hands when everything at its best. However to apply the skill to handle the technology a side branch of wisdom **" skill "** is often used and no one can claim he/she is brainless as brains work and hence walks and machines work and words growing at the speed ever before. A skill is a much awaited term that one is respected with, may be a person is not good at facing problems but the same would be very good at carving others in a piece of paper capturing in his eyes . Wisdom is the basic root for all the source which is never heard or tired of, trying to be a genius is much sure but being a human is much more than everything. When a scholar of philosophy is held with a genius, the genius would bow to the scholar for knowing what life was and has been and that's the power of wisdom then genius.

The sounding intelligence is a power that is expected all over the world but less often to the power of source 'wisdom'. It shall be confessed that I am not against a genius in any part of the concept. But it is the fair will and wishes to explain the world what **wisdom** means.

What would a person do comes running out caught in fire?

What would a person with wisdom do when lost in crowd?

When a person caught in fire?

When a person caught on fire rushes around and with wisdom would run with a blanket and all the pre-cautionary to save the person, whereas an extreme intelligence would run to phone the police about the incident and wait for them to arrive. Who will be better?

When lost in a crowd, wisdom would suppress you seeing the large mobilization, but intelligence would bare you to approach the police for help. Intelligence or wisdom? Wisdom is a freelance knowledge or power which feels free under no obstacles and that's how a failure is brave enough then a topper.

Intelligence safeguards you from all the extreme conditions of life and wisdom would open you up to the world. Let there be a true example, once a road accident on one of the busiest highways of India, a pedestrian was hit by a vehicle.

The population around the incident were interested in seeing the sufferings with all the sophisticated wearing and were bulk minded, whereas a tribal who near passed the incident was brave enough to clear the spot with providing a helping hand to the victim, but sure he was an illiterate and people meowed "Heyy you will be behind bars" but he managed to care none. Here intelligence or wisdom?

A business example here goes to a local merchant with a small business established the hole family into a good condition as ever before, the merchant grew old and son returned with listed certificates of honors in business and marketing and took over the business and unfortunately lost everything. What would this say? An illiterate dad who nourished the business for 50 long years without any heck ups and son got it destroyed only within a span of six months with all the graded certifications.

Wisdom or intelligence? What are you now?

<u>Winning Wisdom</u>

"They knew me but they don't "

"They asked me but never praised me "

"I was told you may be, but you don't exist"

"They called my son further superior than me "

"They gave me nothing "

"They gave me nothing "

"But I gave them what they always wanted "

"They tried and timed me "

"Still I am the same, I call myself wisdom"

Write to the author what you are?

BE WHAT YOU WANT!

Considering the public for a long time, for being the creators of fortunate future is as true as water, but mind it stones always break them apart and the image spears for time being. Running for chances around the circle of life is always a must for landed human and that does not mean in any way to run towards the end of the circle with no edges, it is always a fair choice to conclude, to start and to break. It is a well known tendency of the homosapiens that they never stop seeing those future they always dreamt of, they roam around the universe with free will and transforming time into cash. No one wants to sacrifice their auspicious life for a need which is always wished by others. It is a life running around wheels on the chair and there would be hundreds of steps which plan the future of each, being a parasite in this apparent world would not lead more than being a capsule turning around without edges and sides. Being a consumer for goods is isn't that bad or never but being a consumer for thoughts what people addressed is definitely a one which you may regret tomorrow just blaming those who gave you that path.

It would be very easy when it comes to all the advantages and disadvantages, one thinks in life. After all we are human and that is not enough to get settled with heavy perk even though when you are not satisfied for your own heart, those wordings that are never hosted by your own esteem will be torching out light under the darkness which is typically not listed by anyone around. "Winner many, Loser one " this would be rule of life and should be always since the only wordings that had positive backups would not yield a good rice, sometimes even negatives too are needed. Even then when disadvantages exist and decide to have something which is perfect, effortless. YES! That is good and appreciated, but for how long? Till death? Till funeral?

We are living super powers and the function of the naturality winning and failing is the co-existence of the world is always there and will be, may be the luxury would not be always a pre-vital part but an essential living standards. When it comes to life of humans its not about settling in a few years and passing out the rest as birds, those old saying for the new generation might work but not in a distinct condition, after who else will get all those.?, it is meant for us and we should.

Boxing is a true game with examples what one should always be when staying inside a concrete ring. Here no referee, no opponent, no rules, all you need to do is save you from yourself when being balanced about the frequency of light with no gloves to fight yourself there in the ring. Made rules are kept and you have no points to confuse yourself who I am in those flash lights of fate, those concrete rings are threaded with all the feelings one would be felt and being a disciple observer to those would break the boxer apart from the reality. No audience and no cheering, all you got to do is create your own audience with the power of wisdom and intelligence with tools of skills and lights of vision, all perfect but no one does provide those cheering to battle the war within. Never knowing what the inner enemy attack would be? But you would know how the hero within defends the enemy, realistic ideas and phenomenal calculations containing to docks filled with sand would be time. Respecting time and cause would be seaming to the infinite journey one can travel in those lights called will power. For being what you know and what you want will be disgusting in the early age of life but when it comes to times, when you have to address those smiling faces, you got to have some things, you got to have some things which others do have, but never the mistake of following the footsteps of those ahead since inventions are born only when tried weird not when trying the same after and after. A person would not get a aim such as warriors do, but never less something which posses himself to be that in future is very much necessary than thinking about conditions where he/she can live those luxuries and trouble with a cry of luxury. However the speed and timing of future is may be, however the redeem nature of that future would e when you yourself have got into the boots and ready to walk on, no power of this earth would stop you.

Those with the nature of future would not be blessed with early manufacture of vision but will be presented with a big one that never lasted and that doesn't mean a person is without future. The wheels of life are always not warranted life time, when life itself is not guaranteed, so one individual is left behind.

When you know what others want you to be, its good isn't it? Yes! Right it is very good and admired unless it is your own dream too, being a social animal everyone in this world is allotted with equal amount of opportunities as addressed by all the constitutions all over the world but the sad part starts when a pupate is made and filled a life that of human and asked to do anything. Here the faith and will power are the only paths that one can ever find in the way of dark valley fearing for nothing. The boat sailing around a ocean without the way map is a life where there is no ambition and vision, but once the both are conquered you are left back with a map all over the world travelling across dozens of seas, trucking hundreds of mountains and everlasting green and there would be a chance when hundred of smugglers growing into your region concluding you to be the one with wrong ideologies, take pride in addressing them back with all the response you ever had and have been taking out for years when the light of vision was formed inside you aiming you to be the one among those stars with enormous success and truth.

When those labeled smugglers in real life are those, who come in search of a mind with full of failures to alter the view with free advises on the task performing life which is never considered to theirs, the cheapest and unlimited episodes of people one can get because it is so easy that one gives an advice how to be in future even when nothing bothers them, it is considered to be the easiest way one can terminate others wishes in return.

Dear readers it is phenomenal if nothing such intimacy has not gone through your life and it is really appreciated if so. When you know what you are go ahead! Put nothing into yours, except vision and will power, the highway is yours and one find day those ideas within the vision the society discarded would be called back and the people would love you for that when you have done something which you had in your heart and soul for years, when you have completed it full pledged courage in the same site of society who turned back. Once your task of knowing yourself is done, live the life ever! Ever! Ever!   Keep brimming with peace, wisdom, vision and ideology of future.

"When you know who you are, what you want. It is much better than knowing what others don't need"

Want To Be Me . .

"Raising across with no one in vision"

"Being told to be among the participants which ever lasted with precipitation"

"They gave it a wrath than followed every corner"

"Resembling the society like a mirror whatever gave it o me"

"Seeing around with all the prospective and nothing came up"

"It was the rain in ocean"

"It is the fencing with all boundaries called life"

"Remembrance of past trace of dawn"

"Given the time when it was almost"

"Shed those tears when all tried"

"Shed those tears"

"I came to the light, light of wisdom, light of vision, light of will"

"Four lions across the tide of living life"

Certificate for Humanity

The large extended life on the surface of earth is distinguished by various stages and divisions, but the only thing which always ever remained was the precious term 'Humanity'. The intelligence of human techniques, skills and powers may be anything all around the world and may conquer as many corpus, the wetlands from top to bottom never distinguished any individual based on the divisions created by humans. The basic tendency all around is found with the feeling of guilty and sadness, may one be among the strongest, among the genius or among the most Nobel but the most is never completed without the term humanity.

The modern world which hails from all the anciency is full in new altitude and repulsive force that one can never think for the sake of humanity, following the footsteps of great humanities for the modern world would be like going back to the 18th century, well that is fair enough when people have moved up and resemble the highly advanced world it would be a trouble shoot but the term mentioned is not something which can be altered from generations to generations. It is for those the world today who takes up the prophecy to be the genius and not for the sake of the society, unfortunately the modern world expects everything out of black written numbers across a printed sheet and that would talk their qualities, according to the legends of modern world.

Well but the real qualities are opened only when the individual goes through hard times not by printed sheets, if that was the case $3/4^{th}$ of the world's population would have drown themselves a personality and levels of qualities can only be found during those hard life lines, it trouble and pain wakes up the real individual inside him. As long as rapid expansions are concerned, the lesser the knowledge of humanity. You cant kill a person just because you hold PhD, it sounds cruel. But it is the fact that the modern piece of nature is offered with those considered to be the fallen from heaven and rest from the hell, it is a well known trend in the new generations, you can't tell someone that you are good in humanity and bad at education, people would laugh! But the other can say I am an intelligent and a humanitarian too and you would hear a round loud of applause, this is the fact world facing today.

No one expect some to have humanity excluding all the others, that's not possible in reality because it is expected to have a combo of intelligence and humanity. The sorrow part is when a person attains the so called higher positions, he literally keeps losing the feature of humanity in them and that proves. When visited to country side one can find the pleasure of knowing of love, care and humanity than the ultra modern cities, the real humanity lies there around humans.

With more number of printed blocks one shall not be certified, it is all the inner spirit which aims to have a place in a condition where everything is peaceful and calm with all the happiness. The greatest of the greatest were always gifted with humanitarian saplings and it is not only the term offered to any group of people, it had presence for all the homosapiens and fairly left to decide them to be what.

Unless the term not realized for the better being, it would be no place for humans to live and all this was explained only on a process that humanity is necessary. The humanitarian law applies not only for the humans but to all the living kind, when nature does not believe in distinguishing the living in divisions, why the livings are brought up to do so? In depth the humanitarian law leads to an enormous powerful term holding all nations tight "Peace" since we are assembled to have it only after the law of humanitarian is applied.

"I may be told the dumbest, but was told to live for humanity"

The Rise of futurist

Revolution may start but nothing is going to be alright for sure. The term raising all above and brightening among the stars, the glacier breaks hearing of those calling it **FUTURIST.** A futurist, a one with a bank of thoughts, rays of hope, time in past goes bringing the new era. An era where nothing related to present and nothing related to past, blowing all the thoughts of society which always criticized change.

A futurist the one, the only with peace of mind and hopes for future and thorns in past, he can be with all the critics of the society in past and travelled among them in the speed of light, he was the one who had hundreds of failures in life and thousands of hurdles. He was the one with all the privilege of taking into his mind even after those around him were more terrible than the beast tearing him apart. A clear picture of how enemy would destroy a normal human, but the futurist is clear calm around the time with even enemies; try to peruse a everlasting friendship with a man of vision Mr. Futurist.

As many as sarcastic comments would penetrate into the inner soul of a suicide bag but, he was the one who blamed, who criticized himself, and made fun of himself giving no more choice to others.

There are as many as shrinks and shrill in one's life with everlasting bliss of fate, when all the mountains cried and sky dripped all of them into tears but he shall not fear the wrath of fate, he commands to be creator of his own destination. Everlasting smile, everlasting grace for a cause and trying to convey the best one can do with all power of controlling emotions and readings. He was among those who suffered those days of results, cried all night, saw the stars and went into the everlasting bliss of depression. One who wants to be a "FUTURIST" is not born, he is made time and sequences across life, there are those conditions in which the human being with a sense of future turned into the new era called "FUTURISM" and turned himself among those with a cause evolving to be a futurist. It was the nature's conditions one turn into a time where there is a future for everything and anything around the world and no one would as "what would be your future?

He was the one who saw others as genius and considered himself to be the dumbest alive, he was the one with no expectations and expiry date; he was the one with no guides. All he had was his will and goals people around turn themselves to be the un-interested to interfere into those topics he never came with. There are criticized chances one shall be called "FUTURIST", among the millions of people 95% of them are futurist with the long awaited future, among them every individual has suffered the up beating of failures all along the line of life.

The worlds most destructive was found late and the worst most peaceful atmosphere was also created after a long wait, proving for a right time futurist to admire time wheel. There would be instances where he never knew the meaning of time wheel and never tried of admiring it even in presence of startup failures, but it was assured and punished the futurist to pay it for those long un-admired scenario in past, it is also an very important and impressive quality that a futurist always pays back everything about the past even if it was not rectifiable.

The futurist was too a victim of critical crisis and munch of sufferings too but stood up when it was time for him to stand against the ideologies of the society, not a rivalry but a step towards change in future. The positive attitude towards consequences let everything normal and depends himself from achieving milestone, it is not the real play of getting announced but it is always a work shop hard work from the inner spirit. The life he leads are may be thronged but his will power is never done with what happened. Cloning negativity as among those of comparing identities was never done and so on intensified to begin the mission of achievement.

It must be also told he never took up the feelings in the initial stages as far as the term humanity and peace is concerned, it was a drastic change of mind from clearing the public to make understand what failure does to a human throughout the life. Since then the learning procedure ever started had never seen the board of diversion or end, and that includes the topic of being focused. Even though if it was not a talk of futurist, it is very necessary to mention that the process of learning starts from the womb of the mother and gets rusted in the middle and again gets boosted with a zinc after seeing the cruel face of life and keeps going till the last breadth holds.

The series of haunting in the multi-standard life's never harm a person, it is the behavior which harms them; the talk here is, a futurist was a no saint he too had mistakes and punishments on his way and gave break to those when the horse of black flag flooded his roads. The at most crucial importance for a futurist shall be his tolerance and patience for the cause of thinking, controlling the anger and thoughts is an un-natural tasks but a futurist is an expert in it as he knows how to handle things out of temper. He was a top most philosopher among the small handed group and towards the march for long handed with much better knowledge, it is said to have this quality among each of us for the cause of society to make people know there is life beyond success and failure. This was the idea and confidence of giving philosophical statements always kept him away from the roads calling "failure is a sin".

Friendship plays as a region of oasis in the middle of desert and it gives you everything it has without a second in adoption and doubt, not all are oasis some only it but exist with no land of water to serve the friendship. The once with concern for a bondage live and the rest are burnt telling to leave the room when the futurist turns to them, the only bondage that never concludes will always hope a stay till everything is fine and good and the rest just float, futurist is good enough in finding virtual and apparent oasis.

It was the concept here giving out such examples among the simplest reasons to ensure and assure the every mankind "failure gives power" ad it is told how that power is gained and how it is useless unless it exist within the limits of vision.

"Fear the futurist for none, he shall be among yours, tell him you are not the only one"

Be bold enough to show up the world you are born to be among the super naturals even when doors are shut off.

Futurist they call

"They called me with ego, with negativity when they felt to say so"

"It was the time of dark house and everything let cleared"

"Loyalty was the prime to life through the journey"

"Caring for nothing unless it was time to be cared"

"They gave it with slaps and washed with words"

"They broke it with fear, they gave no time for confidence"

"But I kept the way alive, it is not a sin"

"I grew up it was not so dark"

"Now they call me futurist with one for future"

TRIBUTE,

A gift to all my dear friends for making a journey with me,

It is not about being anti-social for a long time but being very selective when it's friendship. I started the journey with these wishes with me.

Madan H S – *"Be yourself and bang on"*

Danish Hammad – *"Forward reading"*

Arun Kumar – *"I can challenge on you for good"*

Bharath Kumar – *"You are special in things"*

Venkatesh Prasad – *"Do anything unless you are right in "*

Abrar Ul Hasan – *"Bring back those rights"*

Md. Sheik Yaseen – *"I understand the those thoughts of yours write a book"*

Junaid Karrar – *"I am with you"*

Sabira Gul – *"Shouldn't care or give any kind of justification as long as you know you are right at your place"*

Tanu Gowda – *"Trust yourself to be the best"*

Huma Nurain – *"Go to the path which makes you happy"*

Mithin Sagar – *"Tie yourself to your thoughts"*

Chetan Gowda – *"I am there for help"*

Sandeep Reddy – *"Clean surface of hopes for you"*

This would not be a full book without these hands for support.

- ***Bhuvan M***

------------------*THANK YOU*-------------

www.ingramcontent.com/pod-product-compliance
Lightning Source LLC
Chambersburg PA
CBHW020347290526
45785CB00005B/2178